ALVIN ROBERTSON

SWEN NATER

TIM DUNCAN

GEORGE GERVIN

DENNIS RODMAN

DEREK ANDERSON

LARRY KENON

SEAN ELLIOT

ARTIS GILMORE

DAVID ROBINSON

CLIFF HAGAN

AVERY JOHNSON

CREATIVE ● EDUCATION

Published by Creative Education, 123 South Broad Street, Mankato, MN 56001

Creative Education is an imprint of The Creative Company.

Designed by Rita Marshall

Photos by Allsport, AP/Wide World, Rich Kane, NBA Photos, SportsChrome

Library of Congress Cataloging-in-Publication Data

Frisch, Aaron. The history of the San Antonio Spurs / by Aaron Frisch.

p. cm. – (Pro basketball today)   ISBN 1-58341-113-5

1. San Antonio Spurs (Basketball team)—History—

Juvenile literature. [1. San Antonio Spurs (Basketball team)—History.

2. Basketball—History.] I. Title. II. Series.

GV885.52.S26 F75 2001   796.323'64'09764351—dc21   00-047331

First Edition 9 8 7 6 5 4 3 2 1

SAN ANTONIO, TEXAS, IS ONE OF AMERICA'S MOST HISTORIC CITIES.

SHORTLY AFTER THE CITY WAS FOUNDED BY SPANISH

missionaries, it came under Mexican control. In 1836, the people of San

Antonio and their fellow Texans did not want to be ruled by Mexico

any longer and revolted. In a famous battle, 184 Texans holed up in a

San Antonio mission called the Alamo and fought off nearly 5,000

Mexican soldiers for two weeks before the Mexicans captured the fort

and killed the defenders.

Despite the outcome of that battle, Texas did eventually earn its

independence. Today, the restored Alamo still stands in the heart of

5

CLIFF HAGAN

downtown San Antonio, and the city's residents still speak with pride of its brave defenders. In 1973, a National Basketball Association (NBA)

team moved to the "Alamo City." That team, named the San Antonio Spurs, quickly earned a reputation for its fighting spirit as well.

{FROM CHAPS TO SPURS} The Spurs franchise actually started out in Dallas, Texas. The team was found-

6 ed in 1967 and named the Dallas Chaparrals, or "Chaps" for short. One of the original teams in the American Basketball Association (ABA), the Chaps were led in their first two seasons by such fine players as center John Beasley, forward Cincinnatus Powell, guard Ron Boone, and swingman Cliff Hagan, who also served as the team's coach.

The Chaps posted winning records in their first three seasons, but few fans in Dallas were interested in watching them play. In fact, some-

TIM DUNCAN

"The Iceman" overwhelmed opponents with an array of offensive moves in the **'70s**.

GEORGE GERVIN

times fewer than 500 people attended home games. Even after the

team's owners changed the club's name to the Texas Chaparrals and

played home games in Fort Worth and Lubbock in an

attempt to gain statewide fan support, attendance

remained low.

Finally, in 1973, the Chaps were sold to Texas mil-

lionaire Red McCombs, who moved the team to San

Only 134 fans watched as forward Goo Kennedy and the Chaps won their last home game in **1972–73**.

Antonio and renamed it the Spurs. In San Antonio, the team continued **9**

to win and at last became a hit with fans. "We made a few key deals,

won some games, and suddenly we were drawing a crowd," said Spurs

general manager John Begnoz. "We were stunned. People figured we

were geniuses, but we didn't even know what we were doing."

What the Spurs did was acquire two talented players—towering

center Swen Nater and forward George Gervin—from the struggling

GOO KENNEDY

The Spurs
rode high
as a league
power in
both the late
1970s and
late **'90s**.

MALIK ROSE

Virginia Squires franchise early in the 1973–74 season. The lean Gervin, who joined the Spurs at the age of 20, never seemed rattled or overly excited on the court. He was so cool, in fact, that his Virginia teammates had nicknamed him "the Iceman."

The Iceman was an instant star in San Antonio. In his first full season, he led the team in scoring with 23 points per game. With Gervin leading the way, the Spurs went

Swen Nater was the ABA's top rebounder in **1974–75**, grabbing 16 boards a game.

51–33 in 1974–75 and 50–34 the next season. The Spurs were a success, but the ABA was struggling. So, in 1976, the top four ABA teams—the Spurs, New York Nets, Indiana Pacers, and Denver Nuggets—joined the NBA, and the ABA was dissolved.

{HEATING UP WITH "THE ICEMAN"} The Spurs made the playoffs in their first NBA season. Then, in 1977–78, Gervin led the league in scoring with 27 points per game. He became even more

MIKE GALE

dangerous when Spurs coach Doug Moe moved him from forward to guard. Whenever a game was on the line, the Spurs just gave the ball to Gervin. "I consider the game won when Ice has his hands on the ball in

that situation," said San Antonio center Billy Paultz.

The Spurs flew high in 1977–78 and 1978–79, winning their division each season. In 1979, Gervin, Paultz, forward Larry Kenon, and guards James Silas and Mike Gale led the team all the way to the

Eastern Conference Finals, where it fell to the defending NBA champion

Washington Bullets.

In **1981–82**, point guard Johnny Moore led the league with almost 10 assists per game.

In 1980, the Spurs brought in new coach Stan Albeck.

They also moved from the Eastern Conference to the

Western Conference. Little else changed, however. San

Antonio continued to roll as one of the NBA's

14 highest-scoring teams. Unfortunately, the Spurs' lack of playoff success

also remained unchanged. After posting great regular-season records, the

Spurs fell short of the NBA Finals in both 1981 and 1982.

To get Gervin some help, San Antonio traded big men Mark

Olberding and Dave Corzine to the Chicago Bulls in 1982 for 7-foot-2

center Artis Gilmore. Gilmore was one of the NBA's biggest and

strongest players. In Chicago, he had become an All-Star thanks to his

ARTIS GILMORE

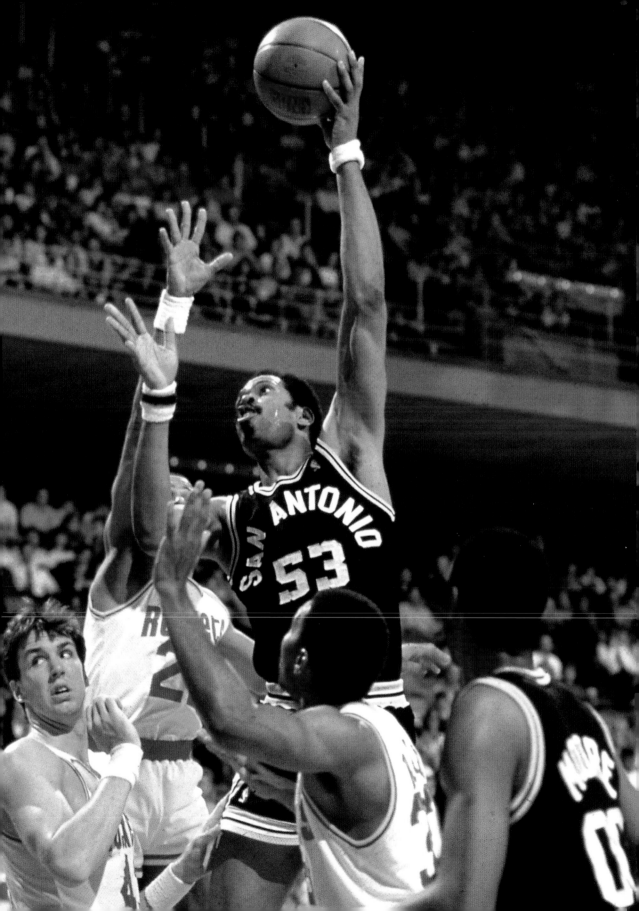

great rebounding and shot-blocking skills.

"But even more than that was the way he intimidated people—the

way [opposing] players came to the middle, saw him, and traveled or threw

the ball away," Chicago Bulls coach Jerry Sloan said of Gilmore. "I remem-

ber Artis going the length of the court and catching a guy from behind and

blocking his shot. Those are things that mean more than points."

At first, Gilmore's addition seemed to be just what San Antonio needed to finally capture a championship. With the big center providing the muscle and Gervin spearheading the offense, the Spurs set a team record by winning 53 regular-season games in 1982–83. In the playoffs, they advanced as far as the Western Conference Finals, where they fell to the Los Angeles Lakers.

Guard Alvin Robertson played brilliantly during some otherwise poor Spurs seasons in the late **'80s**.

In the seasons that followed, however, the Spurs went into a tailspin. Coach Albeck left town, and in 1984, the Spurs missed the playoffs for the first time in their history. In 1985, San Antonio decided to rebuild and traded Gervin to the Chicago Bulls.

{LEAN YEARS IN SAN ANTONIO} Although it was difficult saying good-bye to the Iceman, the Spurs knew they had a player ready to fill the void. That player was young guard Alvin Robertson, a great

ALVIN ROBERTSON

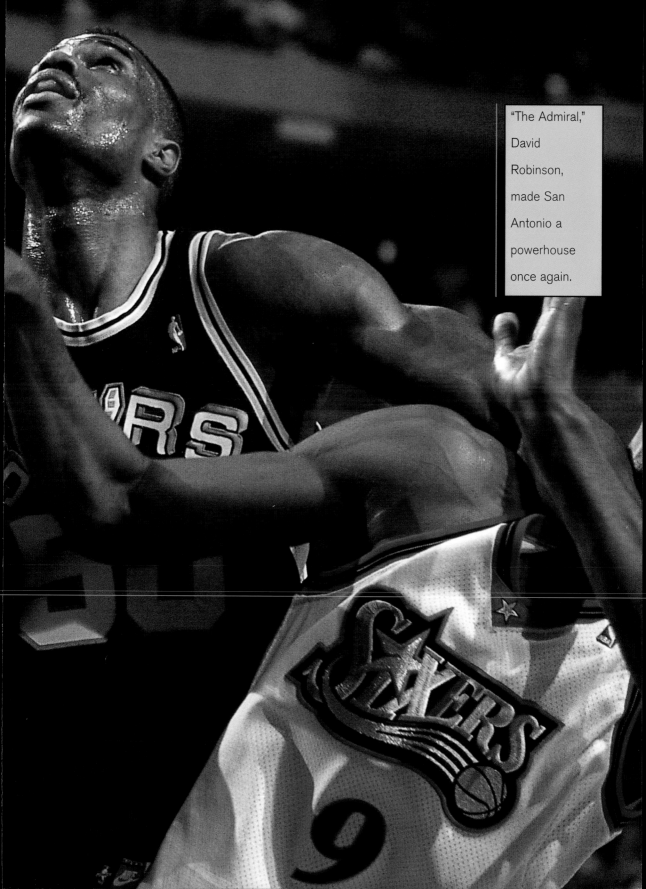

"The Admiral," David Robinson, made San Antonio a powerhouse once again.

athlete known for his ferocious defense. "The Spurs were always known as a high-scoring offensive team led by Ice," said San Antonio coach

Cotton Fitzsimmons. "But we needed toughness and quickness. Alvin gave us that look."

Robertson wasted no time in winning Spurs fans over, scoring 17 points per game in 1985–86. More remarkable, however, was his NBA-record 301 steals that season. For

his efforts, he was named both an All-Star and the league's Defensive Player of the Year. Still, Robertson's achievements did not lead to success for the Spurs, who finished near the bottom of the standings that year and the next.

San Antonio's poor records gave the team the top overall pick in the 1987 NBA Draft. With it, the Spurs selected David Robinson, a 7-foot-1 center from the United States Naval Academy. Even though

JOHNNY DAWKINS

Robinson would be obligated to serve in the armed forces for as long as five years after graduation, the Spurs knew he was worth the wait.

As they awaited Robinson's arrival, the Spurs continued to struggle.

Despite the efforts of such players as Robertson, guards Willie Anderson and Johnny Dawkins, and forward Greg Anderson, the Spurs posted losing records in both 1987–88 and 1988–89.

{**"THE ADMIRAL" COMES ABOARD**} In 1989, the Spurs' fortunes began to change. First, Robinson was released from his naval

duties and joined the team. Then, San Antonio drafted talented forward Sean Elliot from the University of Arizona. The Spurs capped the rebuilding process by trading away Robertson, Dawkins, and Greg Anderson and bringing in two veterans—forward Terry Cummings

Forward Terry Cummings played a big role in the Spurs' NBA-record 35-win improvement in **1989–90**.

and point guard Maurice Cheeks.

Robinson, nicknamed "the Admiral" because of his navy background, used his quickness and remarkable agility to become an instant star. The rookie center racked up an average of 24 points per game to lead the surging Spurs to a 56–26 record in 1989–90. "He has the talent all us big guys only hope and dream for," said Spurs backup center Caldwell Jones. "No other big guy I've ever seen is anywhere near as

TERRY CUMMINGS

Sweet-shooting forward Sean Elliot was a steady offensive force in the **'90s**.

SEAN ELLIOT

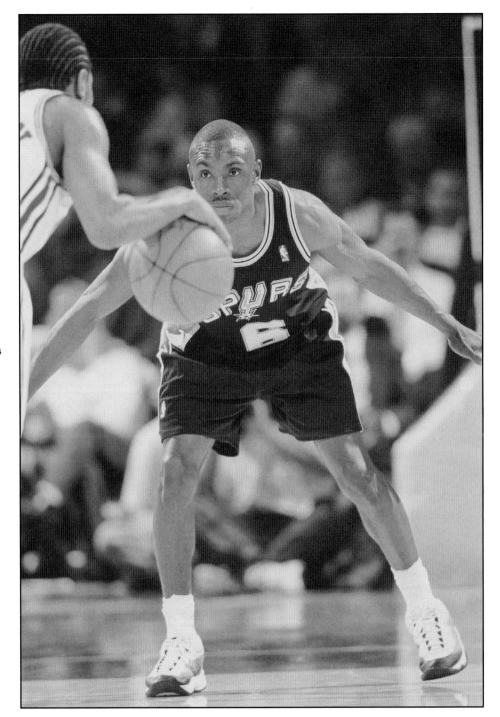

quick and fast as he is. That's what sets David apart."

Over the next two seasons, Robinson continued to establish himself as one of the game's best centers. Elliot also emerged as a star with his sharpshooting and versatility, helping the Spurs to post winning records each year. Both times, however, the team lost in the first round of the playoffs.

Many fans blamed the Spurs' lack of postseason success on their gentle nature. Some accused the team's leaders—particularly the easy-going Robinson—of lacking the aggression and "killer instinct" needed to win tough playoff games. In 1993, San Antonio made a move to bring some fire to the lineup, trading Elliot to the Detroit Pistons for intense forward Dennis Rodman.

Robinson and Rodman could not have been more different. Robinson was one of the league's most straight-laced players; Rodman

AVERY JOHNSON

was covered with tattoos and dyed his hair wild colors. Robinson was

known for his graceful style and offensive skills; Rodman was known for

his scrappy style and defensive skills. About the only thing the two had

in common was their desire to win.

In 1993–94, Robinson scored nearly 30 points per game and

Rodman grabbed 17 boards per game as the teammates led the NBA in both categories. The next year was even better. Rodman again led the league in rebounding, and Robinson was named the NBA's Most Valuable Player. But that was the last season the two would play together. Even though the Spurs went 62–20 and drove as far as the Western Conference Finals, San Antonio decided to make a change. Frustrated by Rodman's eccentric and often disruptive behavior, the team traded him to Chicago.

Despite his eccentric ways, Dennis Rodman was the most dominant rebounder of his era.

Coach Bob Hill, who had joined the team in 1994, then assembled a new lineup that included the Admiral, forward Will Perdue, point guard Avery Johnson, and Elliot, who had returned to the team after just one season in Detroit. Once again, the Spurs posted an impressive record in 1995–96, going 59–23 before losing to the Utah Jazz in the second round of the playoffs.

DENNIS RODMAN

{CHAMPIONS AT LAST} In 1996, Spurs general manager Gregg

Popovich moved to the bench as the team's new coach. Popovich proved

to be a popular leader, but injuries to Robinson, Elliot,

and forward Chuck Person led to a disastrous 20–62

mark—the worst record in franchise history.

That lost season turned out to be a blessing in disguise.

Because of it, the Spurs were given the top overall pick in

In his only
Spurs season
(1996–97),
forward
Dominique
Wilkins netted
18 points
a game.

28

the 1997 NBA Draft, and they used it to take center Tim Duncan from

Wake Forest University. Duncan hailed from the tiny Caribbean island

of St. Croix, where he had excelled as a swimmer in his youth. As a

teen, Duncan turned his attention to basketball, and his skills developed

as quickly as his 7-foot and 260-pound frame.

Like Robinson, Duncan was extremely agile and relied on superb

fundamental skills. Averaging 21 points and 12 rebounds a game at the

DOMINIQUE WILKINS

forward position, the rookie became an instant All-Star. "Once he gets

more comfortable, he's going to be unbelievable," said Robinson. "He

can score on the block, he's got great post moves, [and] he's a great passer."

With Duncan added to the mix, San Antonio leaped to 56–26 in 1997–98. The next season, the Spurs were virtually unstoppable. Robinson, Duncan, and Perdue formed a daunting frontcourt of 7-footers, Elliot and guards Mario Elie and Jaren Jackson provided consistent outside firepower, and the speedy Johnson served as floor general.

Coach Popovich guided this talented lineup to a league-best 37–13 record. Then, in the 1999 playoffs, the Spurs destroyed the Timberwolves, Lakers, Trail Blazers, and Knicks to capture their first NBA championship. "Defense won it for us," said a jubilant Robinson

In **1998–99**, Jaren Jackson helped the Spurs become the first former ABA team to win an NBA title.

29

JAREN JACKSON

Derek Anderson added speed and scoring punch to the Spurs' lineup in **2000–01**.

DEREK ANDERSON

Guard Antonio Daniels was poised to become San Antonio's next floor general.

ANTONIO DANIELS

after the victory. "This championship sends a message that persistence and hard work can pay off."

Although San Antonio came up short in its bid for another championship the next season, the team's future was clearly in good hands—specifically those of Duncan, who grew only more dominant as a scorer, rebounder, and shot blocker. The team also continued loading for the future by adding athletic young guard Derek Anderson in 2000.

Veteran guard Terry Porter's long-range shooting helped the Spurs win their division in **2000–01**.

It took the Spurs 26 years to win their first league championship, but today's team is eager to capture more trophies in the seasons ahead. From the Iceman to the Admiral, the Spurs have featured some of the NBA's finest players. These players and more have given San Antonio a team that never backs down, making it a natural fit in the Alamo City.

TERRY PORTER